Borrowing and Returning

Published in the United States of America by Cherry Lake Publishing
Ann Arbor, Michigan
www.cherrylakepublishing.com

Content Adviser: Danielle Peart, CPA
Reading Adviser: Cecilia Minden, PhD, Literacy expert and children's author
Book Design: Jennifer Wahi
Illustrator: Jeff Bane

Photo Credits: © Monkey Business Images/ Shutterstock.com, 5; © Juriah Mosin/Shutterstock.com, 7; © sirikorn thamniyom/Shutterstock.com, 9; © goodluz/Shutterstock.com, 11; © Natee Meepian/Shutterstock.com, 13; © Phovoir/Shutterstock.com, 15; © Cineberg/Shutterstock.com, 17; © Syda Productions/Shutterstockc.om, 19; © PONG HANDSOME/Shutterstock.com, 21; © Liderina/Shutterstock.com, 23; Cover, 1, 6, 14, 20, Jeff Bane

Library of Congress Cataloging-in-Publication Data

Names: Colby, Jennifer, 1971- author.
Title: Borrowing and returning / by Jennifer Colby.
Description: Ann Arbor : Cherry Lake Publishing, [2018] | Series: My guide to
    money | Includes bibliographical references and index.
Identifiers: LCCN 2018003324| ISBN 9781534128989 (hardcover) | ISBN
    9781534130685 (pdf) | ISBN 9781534132184 (pbk.) | ISBN 9781534133884
    (hosted ebook)
Subjects: LCSH: Credit--Juvenile literature. | Money--Juvenile literature.
Classification: LCC HG3701 .C584 2018 | DDC 332.7--dc23
LC record available at https://lccn.loc.gov/2018003324

Printed in the United States of America
Corporate Graphics

table of contents

About the author: Jennifer Colby is a school librarian in Michigan. She borrows only what she can pay back.

About the illustrator: Jeff Bane and his two business partners own a studio along the American River in Folsom, California, home of the 1849 Gold Rush. When Jeff's not sketching or illustrating for clients, he's either swimming or kayaking in the river to relax.

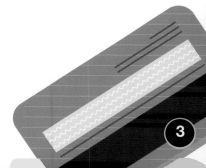

3

Do you want to buy something?

Food and clothes are things we need. New toys are things we might want.

Money buys your needs and wants. What if you don't have enough money?

You can **borrow** money from a bank. It is called a **loan**. Bank loans help people buy houses and cars.

The bank decides if you are a good **risk**. It decides if you will pay back the money.

When should you
get a loan?

A bank might give you
a big loan. It might give you a
small loan. It looks at many
things to decide the amount.

A bank charges **interest**.

Need more time to pay it back? Then you might **owe** the bank more money.

What else do you borrow that needs to be returned?

Be smart. Look at how much money you make. Look at your **expenses**. Borrow only what you know you can pay back.

Have you borrowed money before? Did you pay it back? It is smart to pay back what you owe.

glossary

borrow (BAWR-oh) to use something that belongs to someone else for a little while

expenses (ik-SPENS-iz) the money you spent on something

interest (IN-trist) a fee paid for borrowing money

loan (LOHN) money given that is meant to be paid back

owe (OH) the need to pay money back

risk (RISK) a person who someone judges to be a good or bad choice

index